Common Sense Leadership

Ronald Harper

outskirts
press

Table of Contents

Introduction

Leadership can be summed up in words that emphasize attention onto those that follow. Following is more important than leading. Any organization, sooner or later, will come to terms that it will need to replace the leaders they have with new ones.

The It

Leadership, given its namesake, somehow sustains some perception that what it means is what it's about. It is about all the people that are under it. For leadership to work effectively, a reliable structure must be created that leads those to engage and trust those above them, as well as engage and trust those below them. All, as they handle the power of everything that comes along with it.

The Product

In the accounting world, those that may have been around it too long may not always see its importance relative to all other parts of the company. Accounting would not be needed if it weren't for product or service sales. In many ways, this leads one to wonder about what it is they do, and how it is dependent upon others and what they do. To compare what you do with a coworker undermines the necessity of the structure and the environment with it. Comparisons aren't needed; for the well-being of the company, if one minimizes another's work, they are basically saying, "I don't need them to do 'a good job.'" A level up or a level down does not work well with all that you are working toward. Furthermore, leadership cannot float in air. It needs something substantial to cornerstone what is being built. Leadership is about building. Building a company, a person, and a product. How you lead represents the intangible and tangible aspects of a business and how they all react together.

The Vision

With a useful product, leadership basically gets seed money. In other words, it becomes easier to lead and talk about what is needed and sellable, as opposed to spending time talking about wind chimes. It just simply makes it easier to associate with something that is made of value. Now, to lead everyone who follows a sense of mission or vision is necessary; it connects with the workers who make it, and the people that sell it. The vision is meant to motivate, encourage, inspire, and make lasting impressions on every stakeholder. It is meant to be abstract. A vision doesn't have a goal; it adapts, and changes based upon a timeline that is never meant to end. It's a spirit. When a vision is seen as motivational, it means it was designed with inspired, necessary attention. As I mentioned, a vision is not a goal but rather a feeling. If an objective was meant, a vision wasn't realized. But the vision may have presented inspiration and energy, leading others to accomplish their objective at a faster pace and with a better state of mind. As mind-sets and feelings grow, so will a company. A company's vision is not supposed to go on forever; it progresses to reach even broader and farther. After so long, as people get closer to it, it's time to change it again.

To Sum Up

Now, we have a leader, a product, and a vision. Where do they all fit? And why do they belong there? A reliable structure is led by a leader and a vision. These would go on the top. As the pyramid widens, it separates at various levels. These levels can make or break an entire system. Each level needs to engage and trust the level above it and engage or trust the level below it. What this means may seem different from what it implies. I'll try to explain. By engaging and trusting, one is speaking within a common interest of a company. The boundaries set at this point can fit any given tone. Most notably, they should align themselves with the situation at hand and keep you feeling needed as you achieve for those that need you. By raising your boundaries, you may be delving into a relation of some sort, leaving absent the common interest you are there to uphold. Achievement is the only feeling worth more than the feelings you get from anything bought. Doing what is important to you, others, and the markets is priceless.

By learning how to engage and trust without violating anyone's boundary is crucial to the common interest of a company. Most people can have the best attitudes within a regulated boundary, under a structure that serves as a cohesive unit for everyone. No one is undermining anyone else's job, and others aren't undermining theirs. Each job is important as it becomes interdependent with the jobs of others.

Within each level, some set of management should exemplify what it means to lead the level below them. What this means is that the position they take over has requirements that are more important than the person taking over that position. One's job at this point is to engage and trust those below him or her. Leading through to the next leader is what needs to exemplify leadership. If fellow managers work together but become too important to themselves, they are severing the link of those they lead and breeding ground for fraud or collusion. At this point, the entire structure is in peril.

For example, pretend an owner of a company had told a fellow worker of yours to break down the assembly line so he could call his friend to fix it. In return, his friend would forgive some gambling debt he owes to him. How would you feel sitting there waiting to work again? How important would the work mean to you? Would you feel like you wanted to continue working there? This is what can happen when substantiation or "real advertisement" (or hands-on advertising) is in jeopardy.

Another part of securing a reliable structure has to do with proper uses of power. Power in itself is not harmful to anyone . . . the people that have it, or the people they use it on. Power can be best defined by the ability to influence. The most important question about power is what and how it is being used to influence. The effective uses of power spread it to others. The manager you work for may have power with others with the intention to secure your best interest. Within this scenario, power is also acting as reputability. If used correctly, as mentioned, engagement, trust, care, common interest, and a little fear represent a structure needed to lead others in the right direction.

Other power is based only on fear. If you have ever heard "fear is a form of respect," you know what I am talking about. But reputability based solely upon fear doesn't lead; it acts as a deterrent. People are afraid to engage with their own managers. What is even worse, over time, a management perspective is formed. It states that my workers won't work for me unless they are scared. It also states that my employees don't care if they only respect fear. A reliable structure has been compromised.

CHAPTER 1

A Leader and His Tools

The Right Circle

ONE OF A leader's opportunities or obligations is to maintain a sense of raw energy and to use it to embody a vision, one that shares a common interest of it within an entire company. Raw energy doesn't come easy. But with it, other ways of obtaining it and sharing it become easier than in the past. A common idea that has grown in strength over the last few years is referred to as "circling." Circling is a concept. It is a way of living. Some are positive, and some are negative. Everyone knows the most common circle. It has to do with not feeling good. Often, people that don't feel good do something to get rid of this feeling . . . to find they only feel worse. And they repeat the same cycle. There are many more of these that could be named, but that is not the purpose.

What all leaders should think of doing is encircling in a positive manner. All of us want to achieve. We want to be the best we can be, but somehow, the energy and optimism we had needed blocks us from becoming more of what our determination allows us to be. If you are out of the energy but determined, you may need to achieve or make something good happen to feel better. Then tomorrow, you may be determined to do something and add to what you've done and feel better. Eventually, the acceptance of security through recognition of challenging work and the priceless feedback secures your welfare, leading you to finally let go with a trust that others need you, know you, and trust you. Though you have been encircling in a positive way, many times, this process can take years.

If you ever feel that anything is wrong with your engine, you may find it hard to use to fix itself. "Will" is a "being emotion." The energy blocked because of a lack of will normally can't be released by other "being emotions." But you do have "doing emotions." "Determination" and a "no-quit" attitude can act as your toolbox. With insight, you can use your "doing emotions" to release the energy blocked from your "being emotions."

What you may have wanted all along is to achieve. You can achieve this way. It's a never-ending circle. None of this must be drastic, but if you have too many negative thoughts, find the source and use your determination to fix your engine.

Sharing the Vision

A leader should feel a vision. The vision can be measured by how it makes people feel. If they feel inspired, encouraged, motivated, and good willed, an employer may sense that his vision is affirming to him as a leader. Again, the vision is abstract. It is to fill people with emotions that target a leader's perception of how he can optimize those that work for him. Emotions are energy. By creating and controlling energy the right way, a leader is getting the results that he needs to continue. So, a vision helps to create energy. That alone would be okay, but it needs to be right. It needs substantiation. The vision is not just for the workforce; it spreads to buyers, sellers, and stakeholders. It simply creates the environment and needs to be upheld by a willing desire to make it that way.

Again, leading is less important than those that follow it and need it. They are what is important. The environment you create keeps them energized with what they see beyond the horizon. The concentration upon the vision is not concrete; it is challenging, leading others to want to add to it. The work done and the work to do need to be in alignment with the vision. This is the substantiation of it. Widgets need to be made. But these are not the objective; they aren't the goal; and they aren't the need. The vision that surpasses all of it leads others to engage in its philosophy.

Getting caught up in this philosophy can't help but create a circle. An employee's idea is a reaction to a vision. And an idea is part of a vision. It's part of something bigger, allusive, yet provokes interaction. An employee's idea may begin as an interaction with another's idea: the vision. At that point, employees may engage with thought, opinions, and ideas, furthering the environment needed to optimize what they feel about what they do.

Since a leader's job is only as important as the people that need that leadership, followers begin to feel their importance as well. Their ideas mean something. Ideas are only as important as the use someone else has for them. After you have an idea, it is set on a table, and it can't be yours anymore. Many smart people can use the input from them and create the output to make them work. This is a wish. A common ground has been developed. Contributing to a vision is engaging with thoughts, opinions, and ideas. With the right substance, a vision can sustain any contribution to it. As a hub, anything spoked around it makes sense and can act likewise with contributions.

How to Manage Energy

I believe that many leaders today believe that the less energy that their workers have, the less trouble they have with them. We have lost so many intangible assets over the years that I believe many companies don't invest in workers like they had in the past. They may even hire temporary workers that they know they may replace by the next day. The substantive nature that they had may have been lost somehow and treating a system as a reliable structure just takes too much time and energy. Problems, troubles, and everything else may have seemed to embed themselves into different spots, leaving you to wonder if you can solve any of them. And if you do, another pops up, as if they are a necessity.

A vision creates the hope of an environment. If you did optimize the energy of your workforce, how would you keep them in line? Is there a reason? Yes. Is it worth the time? Yes.

Boundaries

Everyone knows that people talk. The reason for it becomes the answer. Another answer leads one to question what boundaries are and how you keep them.

Most often, the reason people talk has much to do with not doing something else. Substantive nature is needed everywhere. Over time, a vast difference between what we talk about and what we used to talk about has worked itself out from the wood-work. The social media, phone, apps, and more have led us into something that had sold us to it. It is hard to believe that we demanded all this stuff we thought we need-ed. When supply dictates demand, the market is spoiled. We become buyers of what is sold to us and overstep many of our basic needs. This leads us to complacency, and we become victims of our own behaviors.

Basically, a steak is the centerpiece of the table, and we feel it's too hard to eat a cup of spaghetti and meat sauce. This takes less from who we are and creates more exposure to what we see, which begins a relational flaw of talking about people we don't even know. If talking about others is more important than achieving something, we aren't building—we are breaking.

In the workplace, this kind of boundary leaves many caught in something that makes getting anything done less than it should. Boundaries are emotional and phys-ical. God gave us anger to use in a healthy way to protect them. It is your choice and others as well to choose a tight boundary of 1 or 2, or a more social boundary of 4 or 5. Within a working environment, common interest sets a structure in place that can protect it from losing its substance. Common interest, with vision and work, replaces our relational thoughts with those that keep us achieving. Working to produce is a healthy expression of who we are. I often wonder and continue to believe the need of achieving is more important than producing. The opportunities that come keeping us needed and useful will not arise on their own. It may sound counterintuitive, but the steak as the centerpiece needs to be thrown away. Now, the spaghetti and meatballs taste better. We don't need much of what we have. We need to feel good . . . staying behind need . . . to feel good about what we do.

Leveraging against the Downside

Leadership, again, is not about being a leader as much as it is about others that need one. Good leadership doesn't rest upon an intellect, but rather, an emotional awareness and intellect. With that said, much of responding to people may have to do with a sense of where they are at. Managing energy, as mentioned, has to do with proper boundaries within a reliable structure. It also has to do with development of a proper attitude. A leader is not necessarily responsible for his workers and their attitudes but may become aware of them. If wishing and dealing is not the answer, more insight to the matter of attitude development can prove that a matter of perception with the proper control can empower those who would like to extend their leadership capabilities in this manner.

Our senses of touch, taste, smell, hear, and feel constitute what we need to collect stimuli from what is around us. What we recognize as input is sent to our brain awaiting output. For example, to touch something provides stimuli. Those stimuli are sent to our brain. It may be as simple as touching something. In this example, pretend we are looking to buy tile for a kitchen countertop. We may feel a different texture. What we touch sends a signal to our brain, creating a perception that allows us to make sense out of buying one kind of countertop over another.

The perceptions of how we see others is often underestimated. Assessing one another is essential to maximizing one's capability and capacity. What creates a better leader is his or her ability to understand the potential of his or her workforce. This understanding reaches beyond aptitude; it reaches into a combination of intellect and an emotional sense, together, creating a perceptual profile. This profile and its benefits are used to properly associate with one's workers. A perceptual profile can optimize a relation with each worker.

Before I go any further, I would like to better define a leader's relationships with his or her workforce. In order to leverage against the downside, one must quantify what relation is in order to best accomplish this. Personal issues are not part of the quantity. They are part of the distraction from the quantity. When they arise, it is best to maintain a strong boundary. By using this, you are limiting distractions that prevent the well-being of the company. With common interest propelling the relationship, you are relating within common ground beneficial to the company.

For example, if a relationship within a company is based upon common interests of it, a 10 out of 10 would be both knowing all aspects of what they may work toward. In other words, they would be fluent within all aspects of where they work. A leader may know 6–7 out of 10, while an employee may only have common interest in 2–3 out of 10. With recognition, a leader needs to meet each employee within each given interest. A leader must be versatile. A lady in clothing may have different common ground with a leader as opposed to the cashier or bookkeeper. It should be up to the leader to identify those common interests and meet with them within a level familiar to what they do. A company with individual demands of common interests, together with others, is where the water flows the best. In other words, common interests within a company as opposed to with each other can avoid many snags that come between the common goals. Shared motivation toward a common interest is powerful and with a vision . . . unending.

With an optimal perceptualized profile, an understanding exists as to an employee's common interests and an employee's sense of how they relate with it. At this time, a leader's job is still not done. Each worker brings differing personalities. Within these personalities come perspectives about work, compensation, and attitude. Though the first two are important, the last one (attitude) is the energy force that acts as a motivator of the feel-good emotions that prioritize the wants of the company.

Achievement is the only feeling that is worth more than any feeling you get from what you buy. Feeling good about getting things done will replace what comes from doing it. If what one does is important to themselves, others, and the capital sector, the means they use to meet the ends, will be achieving. Achieving is a natural expression of one's welfare. As long as there are more widgets that need to made than in supply, demand dictates the optimal market for working.

Now, given a common interest, a perceptual profile, and achievement, it is up to a leader to work with his workforce and continually try to create the energy needed to work as well as optimize his workforce. Again, one of those areas is to leverage against the downside. This is where psychology, common sense, and logic fit in. And most importantly, to maintain and sustain an environment needed to optimize the well-being of the company. From a leader's point of view, to get what he wants requires this. Energy needs a form of expression, and to control it, leveraging against the downside is used.

What needs to be done is to create a choice. Often, the circumstances and situations of one instance or another leave one without a choice or a choice that, you guessed it, favors the downside. Too many times, leaders may focus on orders and demands and don't always care about how an employee or other employees feel about doing it. They become restricted, told not to talk to one another, and become afraid of losing their jobs. Sometimes, they are often ordered to produce more or produce less. Or, worse yet, told to do what they aren't capable of doing and often are put in situations that are meant to flaw them within the leader's eyes. Given these scenarios, by being set up to fail and knowing that a leader can fire you because you had failed, creates a loss of energy. One begins not to try, loses security, and just doesn't care anymore. This adds to a workforce that just doesn't want to be there. In contrast, some workers are better than others. And if some workers can't work, even without the stresses I had listed above, then the employee, not the leader, has put steps along the way that prove he or she was hoping to get what they wanted: fired.

But has the leader done everything he could to prevent this? Or, basically, is he or she a good leader at all? Maybe the employee turnover rate is too high, and though it's not expected, good employees lose their jobs for nothing at all. By using techniques to leverage against the downside, one can further identify the situation and identify ways of dealing with it. It starts with either a lie or a truth that leads to a situation or circumstance. An employee seems not to care, and a problem is proposed. Instinctively, a leader could fire that employee. But with leverage, a misunderstanding or problem can be worked out immediately, and choices can be given which lead to one quitting or staying. But it's their choice. Now, a worker may use deception or truth to present a problem. The following steps can be used to conclude an outcome.

Assess the issue

The first question that should come to mind when assessing a problem from a leader's perspective is "How many times." Problems are problems and can be solved. But problems that can't be solved tend to become habitual. When an employee has habitual problems, he may not think of solving them; he may only think of creating them.

The next question to ask is "How is this of value." Again, if this is a good employee, a leader should assess the issue and spend the time necessary to problem solve it.

Problem solving (identify the root)

In the next two parts, I will explain how to solve problems and how to make choices. Problems arise every day. To solve them, a choice or choices need to be made. A choice in and of itself does not necessitate a problem. Again, I have used both together as a blend or separated them out accordingly.

When an employee has a problem built upon a deception (what seems true but isn't) or a truth, one must realize that solving it is his responsibility. But you can help him along the way. Most often, sharing his problem will lead him to instinctive beliefs. None of them are true. This is not the leader's responsibility to make a choice or problem solve. Next, the employee doesn't have to solve anything or decide upon anything for the leader to be okay. Lastly, the leader doesn't have to solve anything or decide upon anything to make his employee okay. At this point, there are many approaches you can use to further identify the problem. In a sincerest sense, you may try to find the root of the problem. The five "whys" are often used to get at the root of a problem. By asking "why," one is questioning the validity of the problem at hand. By consecutively asking "why," each answer loses its validity, eventually leading to the initial problem . . . The cause of all of the rest.

Problem solving and choices—leveraging against the downside (the route to the root)

This part of the chapter introduces choice added to problem solving. By solving a problem or making a choice, you are directed to a similar or like-kind concept.

At this point, you have assessed the issue; you have controlled the issue; and you have tried to find the root of the issue or introduced the right side of a choice. Problem solving of itself is solving a problem. Solving the problem is not as important as *how* you solve the problem. In other words, a route of some sort must be used. This is essential to problem solving and making the right choice. Emotionally, by digging some sort of trench from where you were with the problem or indecision, to a point of solving it, imprints a memory. A memory of thoughts and feelings that lead to making the right choice.

A leader's priority by now is to guide the course. The initiation of boundaries at this point are essential. First of all, this is the employee's problem or choice to make. Next, he doesn't have to solve anything or decide upon anything for the leader to be okay. Last, the leader doesn't have to solve anything or decide upon anything to make his employee okay. At this point, the leader has plenty to use. And, no, it isn't his. A leader, at this point, has a big job: to pry out what is in his worker. To pry out his ideas, opinions, common sense, and logic. (More on this later.) This will use what he may not even know is there to solve his own problem.

Now it is time to leverage against the downside. As mentioned before, this could be a true problem or not. To find that out is not the leader's concern. By questioning the truth, you may be accusing him of lying or wanting him to convince you of what you shouldn't be asking. Routing the problem is what is most important. Leveraging the downside begins by creating a choice for the employee that works for you. Honesty is not really what is of the utmost concern right now, since whether this problem is true or not is not what is most important; getting a result is.

Giving a choice to your employee is the essential start of leverage against the downside. What is happening is that a choice regarding a problem could carry as much upside as the downside. Because of this balance, a choice could be made either way. And since this is not about honesty but results, you can use harmless deceptions, little white lies, or the truth. It isn't sharing the problem that counts; it is for the employee to necessitate a choice needed to make either a right decision or a right decision to his problem. In other words, you add whatever (within reason) is needed to break the balance. The balance can be seen as in an imaginative scale. The decisions to choose (by either solving a problem or simply making a choice) are split; half on the left scale and half on the right. A like-kind weight is hung from both scales. You also have two weights to use by adding them to either end of the scale.

To leverage against the downside, one must add another weight to the right side. Or to further leverage, you could add another weight to the right side. Notice the more weights you attach to the right side of the scale, the more it dips below the left side. By allowing perception and direction to your conversation with another person, you can figuratively add weight and lessen favor with the wrong decision (right side), offsetting the left side, which is the right one. By adding problems, issues, negative perceptions, or basically any harmless arsenal (weights) to the right side, how one perceives a choice can change, leaving them a better chance of making the right one.

This same principle can be used to leverage for the upside. This is done by taking weights from the upside without adding them to the downside.

If you believe someone is contemplating a choice that you may think is the wrong one, you can take weights away instead of adding them. This is basically introducing positives, benefits, or common sense through conversion with an attempt of adding favor to the left side or the right choice. Taking weights away from the left will offset the scale in the same manner that adding weights to the right had done.

Although this may feel new to you, it is not too uncommon with what all of this is about . . . "managing energy." By creating the right choices as opposed to the wrong ones, one feels good about what they are doing and where they are going. These feelings generate energy, and they are guided by the right choices that are meant to help direct and manage it.

Validating Achievement

Adding boundaries and leveraging against the downside or leveraging for the upside are all uses to manage energy. With boundaries, working relationships necessitate a common interest. By producing, workers share and relate around that common interest. People that are motivated by the same objectives optimize energy. By expending energy toward a common purpose, the energy spent is managed.

By managing energy with an individual or through a group, you are both building energy and directing it. Both groups and individuals thrive by achieving. Achieving means you are doing something you feel is important to you, others, or the market. In the bigger picture, you have found purpose and meaning. Within the smaller picture, you have an objective or goal. While one adds to a sense of wholeness, the other relays demand. This is where it all starts . . . producing or having something to do. Having more widgets on demand than supply means you can produce. In a nutshell, by producing, you are fulfilling a goal or objective. In other words, you are working through a means to get the ends. And the ends or objective is the sole reason that you have the energy to manage. Since an objective or goal needs to be made, a means to get to that end will automatically fill in. Simply put, by finding something important to you, others, or the capital market, is all you will need to create an objective or goal. By finding the means to meet that goal or objective, you have just found the energy you need to manage. The means of the ends is *achievement*. Creating energy is done through achievement. Managing it matters in how you direct it.

By wanting energy, you want to achieve. Again, by producing, you are in swing with the supply and demand of our capital sector. When you are producing, and people want what you've produced, they are demanding it. You are fulfilling a need. The demand of what you supply drives your producing.

Unfortunately, we are running into situations where supply seems to be dictating supply. That means money is taken out of the market and used for something else. The *achieving aspect* (the only feeling you would pay more for, relative to what you would buy to feel good) has been in depletion and losing ground.

In many ways, the use of science can become addicting. And when we use science, we have to monitor its use. A lot of power was put into producing cell phones and many, many more media outlets. As far as I am concerned, I don't really think it was a need from demand, but rather a supply pushed on demand. When the objective is no longer more important than the means to produce it, you aren't making what demand necessitates. The science side of supply had been built by a means; not of achievement, but one of euphoria, curiosity, experimentation, excitement, etc. What that meant was a lot of science (to make cell phones) didn't come from demand for them, but rather a supply of them. This took money away from what we otherwise would have needed.

Again, when we have more widgets to produce than are on supply, we can produce; producing is a healthy expression of what we need to feel good. At this point, who we are and what we need seem neglected. What we are being sold has been outweighed by the feelings felt by those that make it. Technology and science have been vehicles that carry a heavy dosage of manipulation, overpowering our wants to their desires. I call this skimming the market. It seems to sell what is a fast 15 minutes, a hype, a new thing; something that we think we need but not what we *really* need. The intangibility is not made of substance. The use of it all is a use of what we mostly don't need. Most of what we use creates a social network. By blogging about these networks, we are computer talking an advertisement. The high end is the advertisement; the low end is the substantive value that must substantiate the high end. Within this social media, it often seems the other way around, which makes it unsustainable.

I have talked a little bit about achieving as well as the well-being that comes from that. I have also mentioned to some degree where I believe our economy and the markets seem to be interacting today.

When I mention that the substantiated value is within the low end, I am referring to the grit in all of us to desire something more, something long-term, and something made of substance. That means roots need to be planted. When I refer to achievement, I realize that opportunities need to be created. It is up to all of us to create the opportunities necessary for everyone else.

By achieving, we are generating energy; and when we produce something, we are directing it, thus, controlling its use.

The Bigger Picture

By using boundaries and relating as workers with a common interest, energy is being generated and controlled. When one leverages the downside and achieves, energy is again generated and controlled.

Managing energy is important. It helps to create an atmosphere and an environment that utilizes a leader's interest in his workforce and their well-being. A leader's job at this point is to establish goals and objectives through incentives. But he also has some responsibility to reaffirm the environment that's been produced. That pressure can be alleviated.

The mission statement or vision that I mentioned earlier is essential at this point. It acts as a spirit, or feeling, that complements the leader's ambitions with himself and the people that work for him. It is the hub of the wheel. As the hub of the wheel, everything that spokes from it will prove the same spirit. When you build a mission statement or vision, you are attempting to build something abstract; something that is limitless; and something that circles without an endpoint. An example could read as:

"When you search to be needed, you will always be find a need. As you fulfill it, you can tell everyone else what you have learned along the way."

This doesn't generate energy, but it does help control energy. It helps to flow the energy or feeling in the right direction. When the feelings of achievement, motivation, will, and determination create the energies that are controlled by various tools as mentioned before, the vision takes in with it all of the other feelings as well. It just becomes part of a way people think and feel when they work. It encompasses each employee as a whole.

Bonuses

When it comes to bonuses, it's easy to picture them as a spike in energy. When money is seen as a necessary evil, I don't always understand the necessity of the evil. Money has nothing to do with any issue other than how people feel getting it. Giving a bonus out is a reward or a percent of profit from some sort of completion. In other words, you were effective and efficient. But even with all of the techniques listed above, it may still be hard to keep some employees motivated. If at any time a leader may run into a mundane feeling, maybe an energy spike is needed.

An example might be:

You lead a crew of 10 workers on a Saturday. You tell them they have 8 hours to make 1,000 widgets. When 8 hours is up, they can leave. Now would be a good time to use an energy spike. Instead of telling them how long they have to work, how would they feel if you told them "One thousand widgets need to be made, and you can leave when you are done making them"?

How would those workers feel that entire day? A lot different. They would feel motivated. When they feel motivated and feel good about a possible outcome, an energy spike has changed their attitude about how they feel going into the next week.

These spikes can occasionally be used. But I know by now that many people think it just shouldn't come that easy. In many ways, that leads me to believe that they need to control it because it should never be that easy. Believe me, the "making it easy" road is not the road that this is on. This is the road of "producing for the well-being of achieving and feeling good along the way." Adding adversity to anything you do creates a bad habit.

CHAPTER 2

Understanding Power

IN SHORT, POWER is the ability to influence. Of itself, it is not a "being emotion" or a "doing emotion"; but rather, an adjective. A word that describes a person, place, or thing. Power is often different from one person to the next. In other words, people are made up of many attributes. Some of those attributes resemble what others perceive as "powerful" about someone else. In addition, power is also given to those who represent offices or positions deserving of it . . . from a scientist, a member of the board, a chief financial officer, to the president of the United States. Each of these representations denotes a bushel of attributes that work together and display a source of power. This power can be seen as "to the left" or "to the right." I believe the variations of power can be measured across that spectrum. As you move to the left, power becomes less about people and more about a person. Within its individualistic desires, power often conflicts with others who have power. They may be unwilling to budge; there may be collusion or putting someone in a wrong spot that only you know of . . . controls or groups those within themselves. The tie of a wrong of sorts that each are the only to know keeps them together. But togetherness often breeds suspicion. If they had trusted each other from the beginning and stayed clear of a common wrong, they would have never needed to feel suspicious. Suspicion can root from an issue that is either small or large. For example: offering a free vacation stay for various people to influence them is not really wrong. But if you are limited to seven and exceed that rule, then you have to reach a common ground of a common wrong (which really is not much at all) with everyone who stays there. This bond of "don't tell" keeps people together far better than any oral agreement. This "to the left" power only knows two ways: defeat others who have it and/or make collusions, or create deals. Most often, the reputability of this type of power is built upon fear.

Power can be used differently. This is "to the right" power. As this power measures to the right, every step of it creates a common ground with others, as opposed to overpowering them. Instead of feeling fear, most often, this power adds attributes to its reputability, such as trust, care, interest, and other words that compliment what it means to be deserving of respect. Power within a scientist shares its power with the scientific community. The power given to a member of a board or CEO represents others who are employed and share the same common interest. Even the president uses his power to lead meetings and talk to leaders of other countries. This power represents the common interest of the American people.

When our common interests are shared by those that represent us, we benefit. Power, in effect, is brought to the bargaining table. Each one with it uses it to negotiate and agree on a plan, deal, agreement, etc. None of this is controlling, nor needs to be. Since colluding harvests power that divides and distrusts, its self-serving aspect is never of common interest or agreement. Agreements, on the other hand, are meant to add to a cornerstone or help in one area or another to build one.

CHAPTER 3

Understanding People

The Psychology of People and Business

WHEN ISSUES ARISE, responses are often given. These responses are weighed upon their timeliness as opposed to their worth. The means of an answer is often hurried by the end result of coming up with one. What I've written has nothing to do with decision making. It has to do with a state of mind used to make those decisions. By making a hasty decision—and not necessarily the right one—weeks and months can go by with a type of unraveling until the original problem resurfaces. That extra time used exceeds any time taken to make the right decision.

Whenever I hear of a problem, a number of scenarios come to mind. The psychology behind those scenarios, if brought to light, provides insight. Eventually, those that see a different perception wonder how it could have become like that in the first place. The psychology behind the scenes often provides the answers. I believe it is a leader's job to offer the right perception, making it clear to others that change is inevitable. I haven't held on to anything that is more than 20 years old. With that said, why would we keep an idea, or way of thinking, for that long? A company's priority today must not be restricted to tangible objects or assets. It just is not good enough. In other words, if you had a vault and put stuff in it that may have been unfavorable, the answer is not to cover it up with a further likeness of the same. Instead, loosen it up and let it fade as you develop a positive circle within a faster pace than any of the past catching up to you.

For Goodness' Sake

In many cases, a catch-22 can develop within many areas inside of the workforce. If you continue in a substandard system, the effectiveness and efficiency will continue to drop, and most everything attached to a spoke that prongs from it would go down as well. The second alternative is to stop what you are doing and reevaluate. When this is done, you just may be the only one who sees anything different. Things may become combative. And others will let you know that you had been working just like they had, and they aren't going to change anything. The only way out is to do right for right's sake. In other words, you can't allow yourself to attach your feelings to anyone. Once you do that, a clash is underway. Fighting within a system or nature of a business is always a lost cause.

Put it this way. If you work for a company, and the company is dysfunctional, the system or structure is dysfunctional as well. That becomes the arena. In that arena, in many cases, you will only clash. Dysfunction sends feelings and thinking to all in the workforce. So, everyone is wrong in following them. Wrong vs. wrong leads to ruin. So, in only being right can you identify wrong. You need to be in the right arena to do that. But unfortunately, you can't be the only one. The dysfunction is what is wrong. Being angry at a dynamic will not affect you. You aren't offending anyone or accusing anyone. If you had, you would divide everyone else. Sharing insight into the dysfunction, creating a common enemy with it, and developing a positive circle away from it will do wonders if done correctly.

Understanding Your Workers

A Leader's Job

A leader's job in and of itself will only be a job. But within measure, as with all other jobs, a spectrum can be used to measure the level of aptitude and adaptability displayed by their craft.

Throughout the entirety of my writing, I have been conscious to avoid anything respective of a definite or constant. I've been careful to stay away from labels. Many times, these labels are given; and in one way or another, change with perception and meaning as they are controlled by others. In other words, what they add or take away from it somehow becomes real to others. Whether it is right or not doesn't matter. What matters has become a topic of talk. Anyone's perception of you must be trusted to be accurate. Human beings aren't perfect. Much of what some may think has to do with them and their emotional experiences.

Another issue arises. Many people aren't accepting of change. Why? Because they don't want you to become any different from what they had perceived you to be.

I believe that labels have always been a mistake. As mentioned, people often use them. They identify with what they perceive and label it.

All of what we know to be words are nothing more than other groups of words that are condensed to make sense through another one. Every word that can be used had been made by condensing other ones. What others perceive, in many ways, with many choices, are most often not the right ones. Again, an attitude of this type restricts (knowingly or unknowingly) other people from being different than what they had been, thus, keeping them stagnate.

I believe this will carry an impact on to people. A leader needs to develop. Within this process, most everything is game. A leader also needs to adapt to change. And in some cases needs to change his or her "frame of mind" to do so. Aptitude and adaptability are components of value. They are different to everyone but necessary to nurture.

Understanding societal labels

I would like to mention two kinds of labels. The first is what I had mentioned as "the talk." The other label worth noting has to do with "the warning." Again, "the talk" has much to do with perceptions. More importantly, it also has a lot to do with personalities. In many ways, it's an allowed, learned, or adopted behavior displayed as "insight and collaboration," "control and power," or "entertainment and expression."

Insight and collaboration

Talking about other people is only as good as your perception. People talk about others every day. If done properly, it is neither right nor wrong. Much of it has to do with solidification of another via others and themselves. To fire someone—to hire someone—to trust someone—or even date someone often becomes a discussion with other people. The reasons for this are endless. The intent is not to malign, but to rather understand. One's perspective can often be shared and fed back by another's perspective. A point to remember is that we human beings will never be perfect in our perceptions. The variations of our intent may clarify us. And at that point, what we may say about others no longer becomes the issue. The issue is us and our need to talk about others.

Control and power

To be in control or to be in power can most often be seen in a better light when explained correctly. A strategy and psychology are often the identifiers of their use. Though competition was meant to be healthy for both sides, in many cases, a strategy of some sort may be planned within its process. Running a campaign, playing a sport, competing for a bid, or living in the business world may entail a plan to undermine a competitor. Talk that undermines another is often fair play in this arena.

Control and power can also be used within psychology that often disguises its intention. Some confuse this with gossip. I don't believe it is a positive way to represent your perceptions, but by understanding why may help others distinguish its origin and better understand that an effort can be made to address it, and in some cases, get rid it.

In psychology, two identifiers can often be used to distinguish between functional or dysfunctional. They are security and control. If our home was one that left us feeling insecure or a sense that something is wrong, we might have replaced it with a want of controlling it. Believe it or not, talking about people in this manner is not about gossip or rumors. It is about one's feelings of controlling their environment to feel secure within oneself. Many family roles passed down from yours or my family can be acted out to ensure a sense of security within a different environment. If we had been codependent with members of our own family for the well-being of it and us, we might have already played in a dynamic that needed all of us to be a certain way for another to be all right. We did this to feel secure. As mentioned, we passed down our roles and the dynamics within them to fit in such a way determinant upon the security we would feel from our second family.

Though mostly acted upon within the family, controlling one's security can be acted outside of the family. Controlling how we and others perceive each other is never accurate when it keeps changing. Those that rely upon this security often like you just as much as they can not like you. Without a reason given, this kind of behavior is about controlling to maintain a level of security.

With everything else, a variation or set number of degrees can vary the depth of this and the uses for it. What is noticeable to one or another from one person may remain undetected by the same people from another pursuing the same outcome. This type of control is often misleading. The power that goes along with it can be misleading as well. The power used in this manner is fed from "the talking." This initiates the control that is used by it, leading to a security that is needed to feel.

Entertainment and expression

At other times, people may talk for any reason under the sun. This type of expression may be noted by various magazines and media outlets. "Ratings" are often topics of interest. A sort of entertainment quality is mastered to keep readers and viewers from changing their reading habits or turning the dial.

The warning

Throughout my many years, I often wondered when it was right for others to talk about each other or not talk about each other. I spent some time finding that out. I even wondered about myself. I don't usually talk about people at all but am happy to relate with others based on a common interest for the common good. I had often thought that working together for the good of something greater would lead to energy and increase the likelihood of likability with me, how others perceived me, and how I perceived others. I tried to decipher between gossip and talk. Warning others about one another can be measured by intent. In most cases, a more evasive approach can be used. That would be to set a physical or emotional boundary and hoping that it wouldn't happen again. The rite of the warning can be measured within proportion to the injury. If your fist touches my nose, I should do what I need to protect myself, and based upon the injury, warn others. How this is done can be a hint, a hidden message, or just plain talk.

If I had been at work and somehow or other put a five-dollar bill on the table . . . to find it missing minutes later, in my view, I should move to another seat. But what about the person that takes my seat. Should I warn her or him and how? I don't believe that an ideal solution fits every experience. Most cases are different and deserve the insight necessary to be handled or left alone, based upon each one of us and how we perceive the situation. But I believe there is a difference between looking for trouble and avoiding it. Someone who steals, lies, deceives—or worse—should not be able to continue a habit that effects everyone else. This creates distrust and division. An environment needs to have the ability to work well within a substantive nature. Anything that takes away from that undermines any substance provided by you and other workers that mean well.

Understanding roles and labels

As I mentioned, part of a leader's job is to understand his workers. Although this may contradict the various perceptions that I had noted to be untrusting, I do believe there is a difference between perceiving and understanding. In many cases, perceptions are shown to others and are often sealed within a label that may be helpful . . . but not always helpful to those that are labeled with our perceptions. Understanding other people is neither right nor wrong. The purpose of it is not to label another within the bounds of any like or dislike. It is not meant to keep people constricted to our way of thinking.

Within the workplace, a common interest exists. A substantive common interest. With that entails a purpose or meaning that overrides our ideas, with good intention, from becoming those that would cast upon another some "societal label." A leader's job is to adapt to change. This implies that a vision is in place that welcomes it. Changing an environment or atmosphere for the better constitutes a change of everything that may be spoked from its hub. That includes an attitude that works within the common interest of one's place of work, as well as one's workforce. As said before, understanding one's workforce is part of a leader's job. Again, understanding is never a label; it's not meant to be constant. Within the common interest of the company, it is a tool used to benefit you and those that work for you. By understanding your workers, you understand what you can do to secure their positions and capitalize their potential, allowing them the opportunity to feel good about what they do for themselves, others, and the capital market.

Given the psychological nature of my writing, I believe it's appropriate to categorize those that work for you, to some extent within measure, to better understand how you can enrich them and the work they do for you.

I am also aware that some workers tend to work, what some may say, "too much," while others tend to want everything around them to be a certain way for them to be okay. And some workers just don't care anymore.

Believe it or not, a leader's job is not to find the perfect employee; it is to work with the employees he or she has hired. A common theme in the workplace has a lot to do with social interaction. In other words, getting along with everyone and the dynamics that keep everyone together. I've learned over time that nobody is often better than the next at achieving it. Furthermore, in many cases (within measure), a type of problem, trouble, or conflict seems to show itself as expected, somehow, and in some way. Every day is not the same. To me, the same answer explains what may have happened. Something of substance was missing, leading others to believe that they did not have something more important to do.

Within the realm of business, how to handle these situations often have to do with everything but the people that work for you. But other people don't see it that way. Because of that, our environment has shaped many of us to believe that there is something different about devoting one's time, or length of it, to the same company. This is not the way that it used to be. All of us that want value seem to be exposed to an environment that undermines it. Treating those that work for you as a value to your company can improve over time and shape more than just the place you work. Working with people and understanding them can strengthen a company, allowing all to be enriched by the environment through contributions.

CHAPTER 4

Psychology and Leading People the Right Way

The Overachiever

A BASIC CONCERN that many of us have today is the ability or capacity to effectively manage or lead others in a direction to produce and control. Control is a word that seems to have a feeling relative to what we perceive as being controlled. Too many variations of control lead it to be evasive to us all since its name implies a restrictive nature we often don't want to experience.

Leading and controlling are two ideas that come to mind when I think of managing. Within the nature of what I had written, I don't truly believe that control has a place or a use. When I think of controlling something, I often think that it is because I just can't trust it. If I could trust it, I wouldn't have to control it. Leading, on the other hand, implies that an incentive is in place that directs other people to believe and follow it. I like that word. An incentive can be almost anything. With guidance, many of us can be led along a path that may clarify and better understand what it is that we are wanting. I believe, as I have referred to earlier, that a substance and vision can lead us all to contribute to an environment that enhances our abilities along with those of a leader.

When we feel what we are doing is important to us, others, and the capital market, our ideas about it tend to broaden. A reliable structure can be built. Without the needed substance, unfortunately, battles may ensue over power and control. Without the needed demand for what we do, a juggernaut can tamper with the entire system. Common interests are less identifiable and mostly unshared. Without the need of a structure growing higher through opportunity (economics), a type of crunch leaves all involved with a valid but self-serving concern: ourselves.

An overachiever benefits from opportunity. If opportunity is lacking, alike with many other roles that some of us may categorize within ourselves, an overachiever, in many cases, is misperceived. Many believe that when a worker achieves, a type of alert should sound. A warning is perceived about power and control. An overachiever is not after power. In fact, if given the opportunity to have it, he will most likely share it with others. A contradiction is created. While people sense that an overachiever is trying to reach power, in fact, he is trying to remain *subordinate* to power. By lifting him up, he may react by staying down. An overachiever is after acceptance.

Don't get me wrong, a lot of overachievers have front-end energy and confidence. But to many, the energy and confidence come from doing something important to him or her, others, or the market. Somehow, along the way, "being emotional" had been misplaced or left without understanding. Since determination and a "no-quit attitude" are "doing emotions," an overachiever instinctively relates to getting something done. By doing something, feedback is given. This is not a controlling type of feedback. Many people respect someone who tries hard and works hard. I don't want to imply that assurance is needed. Most often, a family dynamic had led to feelings of acceptance and belonging through doing. The measure of that guidance may vary with any other role. So, left alone and achieving would sprout memories of reinforced feedback needed to keep an overachiever believing through feeling and being.

Again, personalities are a complexity to us all. I believe in most every case when anyone is left unable to do something, they are forfeiting their need for expression. To continue any healthy ideal, most everyone needs to express through producing. The means that they express within this process "fill in" given the nature of the objective. An artist may feel creative, curious, and expressive. A scientist may also feel creative and curious. They may also feel a sense of awe . . . and even a sense of wonder. A worker too needs to express him or herself. By reaching toward an objective, "fill in" feelings are most often feelings of achievement.

When an overachiever has something to do, he may feel a determination to do it, an acceptance from it, and a security felt through memory and feedback. An overachiever wants to feel secure within the structure he is working under. Finally, with time, a positive circle develops, leading one to dispense anything negative through a positive offset. Most of this role can be easily identified.

Security has a lot to do with all of us and what we are willing to give to get it. The timeliness of this pattern can be instilled at an early age. To dispel what others perceive it to be is important. It can be summed up as a percent of oneself that is often misunderstood. Again, all of this may vary; all dynamics and roles are given with measure. I believe we all can get a sense of feeling for ourselves through independence. To need something else to stagnate, to feel good about ourselves creates a codependence. To not be codependent is not betrayal. Whether it feels that way or not again may vary. All people need to express themselves through opportunity, and in getting the help of a leader to do so is nothing other than human.

The Workaholic

A workaholic is a person that works a lot. An important reminder at this point is to remember that everyone is different. All of us are unique with various personalities that are unlike anyone else's. A spectrum must be visualized to understand better that all of us can be measured from one variability to another. With that in mind, we may also tap into our own perceptions, realizing that what we often see and perceive is reliant on us and our emotional experiences.

As mentioned before, many families of origin are orchestrated in such a way to secure themselves and their members. A codependent dynamic is developed for its well-being. This structure often restrains each family member from choosing who they want to be. Instead, it controls them to fit their "puzzle piece" in with the others for the needed picture. In other words, reacting with each other involves boundaries that permit an emotional blending.

Where feelings end and begin are often hard to identify. To be okay often involves a sister, brother, father, or mother, in return, restricting you to be a certain way for them to be okay. How we become from our dynamics can be identified as a family role.

An overachiever and a workaholic may seem to be similar to many of us, but by comparison, are very different. Though they are both roles and identifiers of us and our families of origin, their relatable intent with others is not the same. Though both display an intent to work, an overachiever intends to achieve within a means for wanted security. Though somewhat codependent upon that outcome, an overachiever can fall back within a structure.

Though both a workaholic and overachiever have felt security and reinforcement from working, a workaholic may have identified with working as a "must" to a greater extreme than an overachiever. Energy from working is created through a mindful thought of the past and its reinforcements. Again, what is important to all of us is to have something to do. An environment is very important to every worker. A leader's job is to maintain a circle with a vision to make it practical and productive for all.

The Perfectionist

Again, personalities are very complicated and can leave us all wondering if we are right by feeling we are right about other people. In writing, I want to impress an idea that we all have the ability and capacity to work and do something. But in many ways, an opportunity to do so may be sidetracked, leaving leaders and others thinking less about producing and more about the people that are supposed to be doing it. By identifying some of us in the variation, I hope to address the initial concern. The more needed to be done, the less we feel and think about our workers or fellow workers and how they relate to what they are doing.

A perfectionist, as we all know, strives for perfection. Since it is unable to achieve, they don't often feel that they measure up unless they are coming close to it.

A leader and manager can be very different when it comes to all of us that work for them. I believe the initial reaction in managing workers is to keep them behind the eight ball. To an overachiever that can't achieve and a perfectionist that can't complete their work within an orderly manner, this type of style can feel worse than what many expect. A leader, on the other hand, should see beyond the horizon. A successful environment is one that layers its staff with confidence and security, enabling them to work together within the common interest of their work. It's a tall order, but it is an attribute to anyone available to structure his or her staff within the proper manner.

By understanding some of these categorizations, a leader can share insight into adapting to each of them and how they work together. All perfectionists, again, vary, given the nature of who they are and how they work. Most, though, are codependent, as with others, on something. In this case, it has much to do with the demands that had been placed upon them. Their surroundings must be okay for them to be. A sense of guilt often leads them feeling that a fault of any kind can lead them to where they don't want to feel. This often drives one to perfect what is around them. Religion, eating, cleaning, and other avenues are driven with a true but addicting need to perfect. Any sense of flaw about what you need to be "as perceived" perfect around you may lead a perfectionist to feel a flaw and feel guilt that is not wanted. Within a family of origin, this feeling is mostly tied to a responsibility of another being okay and an amount of guilt used to control another by not striving to feel that way.

As a leader, to understand that a company is built around several types of workers is essential to its success. People that strive to be perfect are often rule bound, sincere, and leaders within their own right. They want to do well for the company they work for and want to be an outstanding worker. They are on time and mostly loyal to the company for which they work. The contribution offered by any worker with a work ethic should not be dismissed but welcomed.

Another Try

In many ways, many of us come across someone that we feel we just can't trust. It isn't us and our perceptions of ourselves that we can't trust. It's others' perceptions of us we can't trust. This leads me to question . . . Is life fair? Is what people say about us right? Is the way we are treated justified? After too much of this, many of us just don't feel like trying anymore. I can relate to those that have just given up.

What is frustrating to me is that what we perceive and what is accurate may be two different things. When a boss comes to us, as workers, explaining why he must close the plant, we may perceive that and have real feelings about it. Though our feelings may be real, what was said may or may not be. So, basically, the stability of the company that we work for may be built upon a perception. In many cases, this type of psychology is used, creating feelings that are true but based upon a half-truth or deception. This type of control can be damaging. Our perceptions are often used as input. This input isn't always based on a complete truth, thus, used as a reason to spend money here or take it away from there. When things are okay, and we perceive them not to be okay, it usually makes something happen.

Again, on a larger note, our perceptions can be used as input. Input to make decisions about what others may think we feel is important. But those perceptions often aren't our own since they have been derived with too much information, too little information, or some incorrect information.

On a smaller scale, I wish we could all understand what it may feel like for someone to be perceived based upon some given information about him or her. If it is inaccurate information, it explains much of what I had mentioned earlier. It provides an answer to why life isn't always fair. It leads us to question what people say about us is all right. It can often act as a tool given to other people to use as an excuse to treat us differently.

Many believe that most of this is harmless. It's not. This way of thinking has promoted division and distrust. I wish instead of believing for the sake of talk, that others would begin to ask, true or untrue, why they would say that about someone.

This creates a bigger picture for us all. Losing a job is very important to all of us. How that can happen to one person or another leaves me to wonder if steps had been taken to prevent that from happening. This leads to hopelessness. The scope of "not working" must be important to us all. To bend a little for the well-being of us all shouldn't be a detriment to a profit or loss.

The point to get across here is that neither luck nor skill is as powerful as a "frame of mind." A leader, given this scenario, may believe differently about firing a worker but rather challenge his environment. This is a test worth passing. By noticing something greater than a profit margin is essential today. Giving someone who is downhearted a chance to work again and providing an atmosphere to promote it speaks volumes.

CHAPTER 5

Supply and Demand

AS EVERYONE CAN remember, supply and demand are used together to dictate a break-even point. When a price is set, and the quantity is set, a point is plotted to mark an intersection. If supply remains the same and demand decreases, the price will fall. But if supply remains the same and demand increases, the price will rise.

What this means is that demand is a healthy expression of our capital markets. The capital market is always changing and can dictate how many workers you need to meet that demand.

A key point to remember is that a company is not built around its workers, but its need of workers is built around the company.

A leader's job is to continue creating an opportunity for his or her workers. A structure must be built with unlimited room to grow. If the potential to produce isn't available, a crunch can occur, pushing production to the sidelines. To avoid this negative effect, two key areas need to be addressed. They are advertisement and substantiation. When you value what you sell, advertisement is a beginning. Sustaining it should be less of a measure than its ability to sell itself. As that happens, legitimacy is proven, adding value to your company. As your company adds value to the market, intangible assets increase. A rooted path is taken, which is linked to a trademark or logo. As substance continues, it will spread its idea to all stakeholders involved. Part of a leader's job is to capitalize on the opportunities at hand. With this mind-set, future opportunities will surface over time.

CHAPTER 6

Conclusion

TO BE A leader is challenging work. The variations among the best will never identically compare to another. Throughout my writing, I had wanted to stay away from any list of traits expected to define one. By giving a list of traits, I would have left others with expectations based upon their worth . . . A want, need, desire, or incentive needed to be in place. If I had done it the right way, it should interest and inspire anyone content to improve what they've already been given. My wish is that your filter creates an output that is of value to you and to other people. As you contribute, I hope you remember what you've done. Then I hope you share it with others. As they contribute, I hope that they remember what they have done as well, sharing it with others along the way.